RSAC

TULSA CITY

D0932251

WELCOME SPEECHES FOR TODAY

Karen Coffee

with Cynthia Gadsden

Abingdon Press
Nashville

WELCOME SPEECHES FOR TODAY

Copyright © 2010 by Abingdon Press

All rights reserved.

No part of this work may be reproduced or transmitted in any form or by any means, electronic or mechanical, including photocopying and recording, or by any information storage or retrieval system, except as may be expressly permitted by the 1976 Copyright Act or in writing from the publisher. Requests for permission can be addressed to Abingdon Press, P.O. Box 801, 201 Eighth Avenue South, Nashville, TN 37202-0801, or e-mailed to permissions@abingdonpress.com.

This book is printed on acid-free paper.

ISBN 978-1-4267-0298-3

Scripture quotations unless otherwise noted are taken from the Holy Bible, NEW INTERNATIONAL VERSION®. Copyright © 1973, 1978, 1984 by International Bible Society. All rights reserved throughout the world. Used by permission of International Bible Society.

Scripture quotations marked "NKJV™" are taken from the New King James Version®. Copyright © 1982 by Thomas Nelson, Inc. Used by permission. All rights reserved.

Scripture quotations marked KJV are taken from the King James or Authorized version of the Bible.

10 11 12 13 14 15 16 17 18 19—10 9 8 7 6 5 4 3 2 1
MANUFACTURED IN THE UNITED STATES OF AMERICA

CONTENTS

INTRODUCTION

The Bamana people, an African group in western Mali, are known throughout the world for their skill with cloth. Cloth making is a community affair where both men and women share the work of its creation. Men are the weavers of the community. The weaving of thread into long, narrow strips of white cloth is an honored traditional skill that is passed from generation to generation—father to son, teacher to apprentice.

Women are responsible for designing and decorating the cloth. After sewing the narrow strips together, women use skills, wisdom, and knowledge that have also been handed down from mother to daughter, teacher to apprentice, to decorate the cloth.

The cloth is colored using mud from the local river. Then, symbols and decorative patterns are combined to create messages of wisdom for the wearer and the entire community. The highly valued cloth that is created is called *bògòlanfini*. We know this cloth by its more common name: *mudcloth*.

The community within an African American church is similar to mudcloth. It too is woven together. In this case, the threads of the community are its people and their shared experiences—their struggles, challenges, triumphs, and achievements. The colorful and festive celebration of special days and occasions conveys and teaches the things of importance to and within the community, such as traditions, values, and love. Like mudcloth, African American special days tie the people together while reminding them of their history and heritage.

Through the celebration of milestones and the honoring of accomplishments, the values and beliefs of the African American Christian faith are shared. These celebrations provide teachings and wisdom that encourage certain standards of behavior and traditions that are beneficial for the individuals as well as the entire church community.

Welcome Speeches for Today is a tool that offers introductory words for just such special days and occasions. As the first words that guests, friends, and worshipers hear, the welcome is an essential aspect of any celebration, special day, or program. It not only extends hospitality but also invites those in attendance into a community that believes in and shares God's eternal truths and unconditional love.

Throughout this book, writing spaces are provided to allow you to tailor the material to your specific church or celebration. The statements and prayers that are included can be adapted for each church program or occasion by adding dates, places, the name of your church, or the names of honorees and other church members, where appropriate.

WELCOME WORDS FOR ANY OCCASION

WELCOME

Good morning, church! It is truly good to find ourselves once again in this house of praise, this place of worship and celebration of God's presence in our lives. We are grateful to celebrate the _____ today. Let us go to the throne in prayer.

God, coming as humbly as I know how, I have heard your voice speaking to me, and Lord, I ask that you grant me utterance now to speak your word. Create in your children clean hearts, that we may have planted in our soil seeds this day that will grow high and bear great fruits. I ask this in the name of your precious son, Jesus Christ. Amen.

WELCOME

Welcome to _____. It is gratifying to see such a large gathering here today (this morning, afternoon, evening). We are grateful for the opportunity now to hear from _____ about _____, and for the opportunity to ask questions.

WELCOME

Good (*morning, afternoon, evening*)! We are blessed that we are able once again to gather as a community in God's house. Welcome to everyone present today. May we keep our minds and hearts open as we receive God's word this day.

WELCOME

Leader: On behalf of our pastor, _____, we extend a warm and joyous welcome. We are pleased that you have come to worship in the name of our Lord and Savior, Jesus Christ, who continues to bless us each and every day.

All: Thanks be to God for those kind words of welcome. May the presence of God bless this house of worship and all of us who gather here today.

WELCOME

Leader: On this _____, we celebrate the _____. We are pleased that you have come to share in this special occasion with us here at _____.

All: We accept your kind words of welcome. We are honored to be here today, and we thank you for making us feel so welcomed and at home.

WELCOME

Greetings to our members, visitors, and friends who have come to celebrate with us during our _____. On behalf of our pastor, _____, we thank you for coming.

We are grateful for our special guests who were invited to share with us in ministry. God bless _____ for graciously agreeing to be here today. We welcome you and pray that you will be blessed during our time together.

WELCOME

Make a joyful noise unto the Lord! This is a great day to praise God through celebration, song, and worship. We welcome everyone who has come to join us today. We ask God to bless those of us gathered together so that we might bless others. Thank you for coming.

WELCOME

Hello, friends! Welcome to _____. We are happy to see the smiling faces of so many friends and family. To our guests, we ask that you let us know if we can make your visit more pleasant. We pray that God will bless you during your time with us and keep you as you leave this place. Again, welcome.

WELCOME

Welcome, everyone! We have saved a seat for you at God's table. We invite you to join us as we worship and praise God. Friends and strangers, as well as members of the church, are always welcome at God's table in God's house. We here at _____ say, "Welcome."

WELCOME

Rejoice and be glad, this is the day that the Lord has made! We extend sincere greetings to everyone gathered here today as we celebrate and honor a living and loving God. May you feel God's presence throughout your visit here at _____.
May God's grace bless you today and always. Welcome!

WELCOME

Our doors are open, and we are glad that you have chosen to come in! We welcome you as we sing and praise God. Know that when we gather in God's house, God's people are always welcome. On behalf of _____, I welcome you.

WELCOME

Welcome, church members, friends, and visitors! We here at
_____ are pleased that you have chosen to join
us today in the presence of our Lord and Savior, Jesus Christ.

WELCOME SPEECHES FOR SPECIAL DAYS AND OCCASIONS

MOTHER'S DAY

We welcome all today on this Mother's Day: those who are mothers, those who fill the role of mother, and those who are honoring our mothers.

This is a gathering filled with love: our love of Jesus, our love from our mothers, and our love for our mothers. Mothers do so much for their children, family, friends, and community. God loves and blesses a cheerful giver.

Turn to your mother, or any mother, and say one of the following:

> "I love you, Mother!"
> "You are a wonderful mother!"
> "I am glad you are my mother!"
> "Thanks for being my mother!"

(All mothers, mothers-to-be, and grandmothers can be given a rose that shows gratitude for all they do for their families, friends, and community.)

We wish you a glorious day today!

Prayer

Wonderful God, thank you for our mothers, biological and chosen. Where would we be without a mother's loving guidance? Bless our mothers as they bless us with their wisdom and compassionate insight. As they care for us and others, remind them also to care for themselves. Thank you for the strong and caring women whom we call Mother. Amen.

Suggested Scripture

Honor your father and your mother, so that you may live long in the land the LORD your God is giving you. (Exodus 20:12)

WOMEN'S DAY

A WOMAN is: a mama *and* a business owner or partner. A sister or grandmother *and* a community activist or organizer. A niece or aunt *and* an entrepreneur, laborer, or professional.

A WOMAN is: the head of her household or a partner with her husband at home or work. A sista-friend *and* the chair of a committee at church. An executive or team leader at work *and* a great cook.

A WOMAN can: support the weight of a family *and* ask for help when she needs it. She is a confidant *and* a confider. She is marshmallow sweet with loved ones *and* hard as a hammer head with loved ones.

A WOMAN is: a multifaceted jewel, both tough and rare. She lives a life that is full, rounded, and whole-bodied. She knows joy and disappointment, challenges and triumphs. Married or single, professional or skilled worker, twenty-two or ninety-two, a WOMAN is a gift from God.

On this special day, we welcome and honor our gifts from God—those who are members of our church community as well as others who have chosen to celebrate with us today. We hope that you will be touched by the words and actions shared today and experience the love extended to all every day.

Prayer

Gracious and wonder-filled God, we pray for women everywhere. Thank you for the women in our lives, and for those we have yet to meet. Let them live healthy and well every day—courageous and strong in the knowledge that with you all things are possible, all mountains movable, and all challenges surpassable. With melodious song, quiet determination, or insistent voice, they bless our lives and world. With brilliance and beauty they take on challenges mountainous or minor that bring your kingdom on earth closer to fruition. Always and in all ways, we give you thanks. Amen.

Suggested Scripture

She is clothed with strength and dignity;
    she can laugh at the days to come. (Proverbs 31:25)

FATHER'S DAY

WELCOME, fathers, this is your day.

Today we joyfully acknowledge our appreciation for you. Fathers, we want each of you to know that you are appreciated by your family, friends, and community. What a special blessing we have received by knowing and loving gifted, caring, and strong Christian men, like you, who serve the Lord!

Sometimes we take fathers for granted. Society encourages us to see fathers as strong providers who lack sentiment and feelings. We, however, know differently. Looking at the congregation, I see fathers who are strong yet also loving, nurturing, encouraging, and responsible. I see fathers who not only are capable and responsible providers financially but also are of the Christian faith and tradition. I see fathers who care deeply about their families, their God, their church, and their community.

To the young males who are present today, we ask that you follow in the footsteps of your father or one of the other fathers around you. There are excellent role models in our midst—men who are educated, who respect and support the women and girls in their lives, who create businesses or work at jobs they enjoy, and who work and contribute to their community. We thank God for these men of honor, our fathers!

Prayer

Fathers, we pray that God will continue to bless each of you with health, strength, and happiness. What a tremendous blessing to have spirited, committed, and compassionate Christian men like you here at _____.

On behalf of the women, children, members, and friends of _____, I thank you for your faith, dedication, and hard work in a world that too often overlooks your disciplined commitment. May God's abundance shower you today, tomorrow, and forever. Amen.

Suggested Scripture

The steps of a good man are ordered by the LORD,
And He delights in his way. (Psalm 37:23 NKJV™)

MEN'S DAY

Today we celebrate the men in our lives. Men who, with strength, love, and patience, teach and encourage us on this journey of life. We celebrate the way you lovingly care for your families, friends, church, and community.

Men of _____, we don't say thank you often enough. Thank you for your exceptional, wonderful magnificence. These are words not often associated with men. Too often we hear words such as *tough, harsh, aggressive, arrogant, cool*, and *insensitive*. It's time, though, to move away from Hollywood's definition of men, a definition that doesn't fit our experience of men. From personal experience, we know that men are tough *and* caring, strong *and* nurturing, proud *and* thoughtful, aggressive *and* compassionate.

Thank you for being men we can lean on and into for support. Thank you for being men whom we love and cherish. Thank you for being men of strength, wisdom, responsibility, and laughter. Thank you for making our lives richer for knowing and loving you. Thank you for simply being you.

Prayer

Loving God, we ask your blessings on the men of this world. Too often they are burdened with labels that do not fit and problems they did not create. Help us broaden our vocabulary of men, so that we see the whole man and all that he does and is. We pray that you will bless each man present today with good health in body, spirit, and mind. We ask that each man will feel your loving guidance and embrace, in all things and in all ways. Amen.

Suggested Scripture

He prays to God and finds favor with him,
   he sees God's face and shouts for joy;
   he is restored by God to his righteous state. (Job 33:26)

FAMILY DAY

Families are wonderful because they come in all shapes, sizes, and configurations—one parent or two parents raising children, a grandparent raising grandchildren, adult children and a parent, a sibling raising a sibling, adoptive parents and an adoptive child, aunts or uncles raising nieces and nephews, friends raising friends' children, a stepparent raising stepchildren, and so on. Regardless of the way a family is knitted together—by blood or choice—families, at their best, provide love, support, and stability to one another.

Families teach us how to love, share, cooperate, and live with one another. They provide a foundation on which we build our lives. They help us learn what and who is valued and treasured. They teach us who we are and whose we are.

What a marvelous day that has been given us! Families, we welcome you to this special celebration. This Family Day affirms what is important in life—fathers, mothers, children, babies, grandparents, brothers, sisters, aunts, uncles, nieces, nephews, cousins, other relatives, visitors, and friends.

Prayer

God of love and wonder, thank you for this day of celebration and family. In love we come together as husbands and wives, fathers and mothers, children, extended family, and friends. Thank you for allowing us to celebrate this day of fun, happiness, sharing, caring, love, and forgiveness. Help us pass our traditions of faith and love for you and for one another to each member of our family. Bless every member of our family—whether biological, chosen, or worldwide—with your caring compassion. Help us remember that together we are strong and that our strength comes from you. Amen.

Suggested Scripture

Only be careful, and watch yourselves closely so that you do not forget the things your eyes have seen or let them slip from your heart as long as you live. Teach them to your children and to their children after them. (Deuteronomy 4:9)

PASTOR ANNIVERSARY/ APPRECIATION

Welcome, family and friends, to the day we honor our pastor, _____. Today's celebration would be incomplete without also celebrating the pastor's family, including _____. We are grateful for the gifts that each of you was given by God and for the way you choose to use those gifts to benefit yourselves and our worshiping community.

Pastor _____, we celebrate who you are and what you do. We honor your gifts, vision, talents, and service to God through your work here at _____.

Though we are all servant leaders, we celebrate the leadership of Pastor _____, leadership that has helped us grow as individuals and as a collective faith body. Thank you for your service to God, the church family, and the larger community. Thank you for the neighbors and friends you touch inside the church walls, throughout the neighborhood, and beyond any horizon that our eyes can see.

Prayer

God, we are humbled by your awesome power. We acknowledge with gratitude the shower of blessings we have received through the pastoral leadership of _____. We pray that our work together will continue to enhance your vision of your world. We pray for the spiritual, mental, and physical well-being of our pastor and (*his/her*) family. Keep all members of the church within your loving, protective embrace. Help us know that we are always loved, even when we sometimes act unloving. Give us patience with one another to realize the fulfillment of your vision for each of us. For these gifts and all others you bestow, we say thank you. Amen.

Suggested Scripture

Then I will give you shepherds after my own heart, who will lead you with knowledge and understanding. (Jeremiah 3:15)

LEADER APPRECIATION

Today we are honoring the leaders of _____.
Although churches are composed of individuals, much of God's work is done through a collective effort through those individuals, and a collective effort would not be possible without good leaders.

Leadership requires a balance of gifts such as organizing, envisioning, and planning, along with compassion, team building, and encouragement.

Leaders, we would like to thank you for your willingness to share your individual gifts with us and to serve in a capacity that we know can be both challenging and rewarding. We are grateful for the unique gifts that each of you contributes to _____.

Prayer

God, each of us is called to servant leadership in your church. Some of us are called to chair a committee, lead a group, or spearhead an event. We thank you for the members of _____ who have committed to this service. We pray for your guidance in every idea that is considered, every plan that is executed, and every decision that is made. Amen.

Suggested Scripture

He chose capable men from all Israel and made them leaders of the people. (Exodus 18:25)

AFRICAN AMERICAN HISTORY DAY/PROGRAM

This is a time to celebrate our legacy, culture, and heritage.

This is a time to celebrate our history as African Americans in America.

This is a time to celebrate American history through the history of African Americans.

Although we have designated only one day for our celebration together, we recognize that African American history occurs and occurred 365 days a year. We use this time of study and remembrance not to glorify the past but to honor and celebrate who we are as a people and a community. In a culture that idolizes youth and instant gratification, it is important to take the time to reflect and remember that the *present* also includes a *past*.

As we celebrate our cultural history, the lessons from the past become fertile soil for the future. In that future the vision of the ancestors will continue to be realized as we grow, prosper, and flower to full bloom as individuals, a community, and a society.

Prayer

Dear Lord, during this celebration of African American history, we gratefully acknowledge our past—even the most trying, hurtful, and challenging periods. We honor our ancestors' past triumphs and tragedies. We look back and discover the depth and breadth of our people, heritage, and community. We stand firm in a heritage of African and African American strength, creativity, intellect, and spirituality. We ask you to help us remember who and whose we are and then use that knowledge as bread for the journey ahead. Amen.

Suggested Scripture

And we know that all things work together for good to those who love God. (Romans 8:28 NKJV™)

HOMECOMING/
CHURCH ANNIVERSARY

Welcome, family, friends, and guests, to _____!

Today we celebrate our church's heritage. A congregation is composed of its members, its leaders, and their work and service to one another and the community. Proudly, we honor our church's work and presence in this community and city since *(founding date)*. We are God's people striving to do God's will always and in all ways.

Thank you to our members, past and present, who have come home to visit and celebrate. On this *(number)* anniversary of our congregation, we are grateful to have the family back together. We extend a joyous, soul-filled welcome to our friends and visitors who have chosen to celebrate this day with us. Our hope is that you will feel welcomed into God's embrace through our celebration of *(church name)*.

Prayer

O God of glory, we praise you with thanks and gratitude. We celebrate and honor you through this celebration of *(church name)*. The rich heritage of this church is a result of a legacy of hard work and service in your name. You have blessed us many times over, and we in turn strive to be a blessing many times over. Help us remember that service is more valued than the servant. As we move forward from this day, remind us to keep you as the focus of what we think, say, and do. In the God that makes all things possible, amen.

Suggested Scripture

Blessed are they that dwell in thy house: they will be still praising thee. (Psalm 84:4 KJV)

GRADUATION RECOGNITION

We are pleased that you could join us for our service celebrating our graduates today. Our *(number)* graduates demonstrate *(church name)* commitment to education and achievement.

Let us thank God for the blessing of ability that each of our graduates has shown. As a church we have watched each graduate grow and mature. With encouragement, we, along with your parents, family, and friends, have prayed for your safe passage through each phase of your development and education.

Graduates, our prayer is that God will continue to bless you as you move forward in the world toward your next challenge. May you experience many more accomplishments on your life's journey. Graduates, we are proud of you, and we honor your achievements.

Prayer

God, bless our graduates. They have demonstrated focus, perseverance, hard work, and determination. They have faced and met the scholastic goals before them. Help them retain the lessons they have learned and effectively use them in the future. Remind them that the acquiring of knowledge and wisdom is a continual process.

Keep us mindful of your continued presence in our lives, regardless of the challenge or triumph. We give thanks to the One who bestows all gifts. Amen.

Suggested Scripture

Ye are the light of the world. A city that is set on a hill cannot be hid.

Neither do men light a candle, and put it under a bushel, but on a candlestick; and it giveth light unto all that are in the house.

Let your light so shine before men, that they may see your good works, and glorify your Father which is in heaven. (Matthew 5:14-16 KJV)

PRESCHOOL GRADUATION

Welcome to our program for the graduates of our preschool.

This year our _____ students are off to a great start. Parents and guardians, we congratulate you also on this first milestone in your child's education.

Children, we are so proud of you. We challenge each of you to live your life so that you will always be proud of yourself.

Friends, family, and visitors, let us celebrate our young graduates!

KINDERGARTEN GRADUATION

Welcome, friends and family, to our kindergarten graduation! Thank you for being here to share this special day with us.

Our young graduates look beautiful and handsome as we honor them today. This has been a busy year of learning, sharing, and growing. For their hard work, we honor and celebrate our kindergarten graduates. As this door closes, another opens toward the next step in their education.

Graduates, we love you and are proud of your accomplishments. God bless you.

MIDDLE SCHOOL GRADUATION

Welcome! It is great that so many parents, friends, and families have joined us to honor our middle school graduates.

Graduates, you have completed *(number)* years at your various schools and are now ready to move to high school. Middle school was fun but challenging. It brought more independence; different classes and teachers; teenage benefits and problems; and new ways of dealing with friends, parents, and adults.

You have met these challenges, and we are proud of you. Class of _____, we celebrate your achievement.

HIGH SCHOOL GRADUATION

Welcome, parents, friends, and families of the graduates of
_____.

Congratulations, graduates! We celebrate each of you upon accomplishing this major milestone. You are ready for the next phase of your life: college, work, marriage and family, or preparing for another dream or goal.

Today, in our uncertain world, we take pride in your commitment to your education and in your traveling the road ahead. May God continue to bless your efforts as you strive toward your dreams and future goals. Remember that with God, no obstacle is too big and no mountain is too high.

Again, we welcome everyone to our program honoring our high school graduates.

CHILDREN'S DAY

Welcome, everyone! This is Children's Day—a day when we celebrate God's youngest gifts. To our visitors and friends, we thank you for being here today and for choosing to share this special time with us.

Welcome to all the little children—our precious ones, our "Mini-Me"s, our offspring and gifts from God.

Today, we celebrate you. We want you to know how much you mean to us, so this is your special day. Through our love, we accept the responsibility for creating a happy and safe environment that will help you grow into the best and brightest flower you can become.

Childhood is a time to play, explore, and learn about the world. On this Children's Day, we remember that our children here at _____ are but a few of the millions of children in the world. Although some children observe traditions different from our own, we remember and celebrate all children as members of the family of God.

Prayer

Thank you, God, for our children, your wise and wonderful blessings. Help us nurture and care for them as carefully as we would tender young plants. We celebrate each child in our midst and their unique gifts. Help us remember that these are just a few of your children. Bless and keep all of your children safe from harm—those close by and those who live on the other side of the world. As we raise and work with children, help us to learn as much as we teach, to hear as much as we tell, and to love more than we discipline. Amen.

Suggested Scripture

Suffer little children to come unto me, and forbid them not: for of such is the kingdom of God. (Luke 18:16 KJV)

YOUTH SUNDAY

Our children are a precious gift from God. We have watched them grow day by day. We have witnessed the changes in them physically, mentally, and spiritually. We have supported and encouraged them through their struggles, and we have witnessed every milestone. We recognize their accomplishments because we were there cheering, offering advice, teaching, and praying during every step. Their family, friends, and faith community provided a steadying hand when they were two, twelve, or twenty-two.

On behalf of _____, we are pleased to have you come to worship and celebrate with us today.

Our youth are busy and involved in a number of activities at church, school, and the community at large. They participate in *(scouting, sports, chess, debate, dance, karate, volunteering and so on)*. We celebrate and honor our dedicated and faith-filled young people.

Prayer

With joy and gladness, we give thanks for our youth. We have watched them grow from children into disciplined, committed, faithful young servants of God. Thank you, God, for their gifts, talent, and spirited exuberance. We ask that you continue to bless them. Shine your light of grace and wisdom upon their lives. Guide their paths in the way you would have them live, and may they honor you. Amen.

Suggested Scripture

The lines are fallen unto me in pleasant places; yea, I have a goodly heritage. (Psalm 16:6 KJV)

YOUNG ADULTS

Today we celebrate young adults. Too often after graduation, they go unnoticed until they are older or more established in their careers. Thank you for joining us today as we recognize and honor the young adults of _____.

Young adults, we celebrate you today. You are a diverse group. Some of you have recently graduated from high school or college. Others of you may have been working for a while. Some of you may be single, and some of you may have married and started families. The age differences, experiences, and interests of young adults are as varied as the individuals themselves.

We want you to know that we recognize your wealth of talent and your range of experience. We thank God for them. We appreciate who you are and all that you contribute through your faithful service and work for the church and for God's kingdom.

God bless our young adults!

Prayer

Gracious God, we come to you in thanksgiving and praise. Bless each of our young adults. Comfort and care for them as they face the triumphs and challenges that come with this stage of their lives.

Help all of us remember our own experiences at that age and offer encouragement and love when needed. Guide their thoughts and actions in ways that honor themselves and you. Amen.

Suggested Scripture

The lines are fallen unto me in pleasant places; yea, I have a goodly heritage. (Psalm 16:6 KJV)

MARTIN LUTHER KING, JR. TRIBUTE

Welcome, friends! Today we pay tribute to the Reverend Dr. Martin Luther King, Jr. We are glad you have joined us to celebrate his life and honor his work. His "I Have A Dream" speech ignited a fire that continues to burn today—a dream that offered a vision that many could not imagine until the election of Barack Obama as the forty-fourth president of the United States of America.

President Obama channeled that fire into a you-must-help spirit throughout the country, serving as a powerful reminder to us of Dr. King's dream and that we can accomplish anything we dare to dream.

During Barack Obama's campaign and election, we witnessed a resurgence of pride within the Black community and throughout the country. People refused to accept the notion that skin tone is an indicator of qualification for the job of president. This was Dr. King's dream in action: people of every skin tone moving past race and uniting for a common goal.

Today, we honor Dr. Martin Luther King, Jr., and the cause he lived and died for.

Prayer

God of glory and infinite wisdom, you see a future that we cannot imagine. Since we cannot see your future, we believe it can't happen. But you know otherwise, God. Help us channel our disbelief into faithful work and service, realizing that your will is not revealed all at once, but bit by bit. Thank you for the life and work of Dr. Martin Luther King, Jr., and for all of those who believed in and worked to make his dream a reality. Help each of us accept your call to do our part to bring your vision of America and the world to fruition. In gratitude and love we give you thanks. Amen.

Suggested Scripture

For there is hope of a tree, if it be cut down, that it will sprout again, and that the tender branch thereof will not cease.

Though the root thereof wax old in the earth, and the stock thereof die in the ground;

Yet through the scent of water it will bud, and bring forth boughs like a plant. (Job 14:7-9 KJV)

PRAYERS AND POEMS

GOD IS THERE

God, every time I call,
You are always there.
I tell you the secrets
Of my heart,
And with open ears
My problems
Always you do hear.
No matter what I do,
Think, feel or say
You are always present
To give me support
Each and every day

Karen Lynn Coffee

MOTHER

M – Makes others a priority
O – Overhears everything
T – Takes the bitter with the sweet
H – Helps others
E – Encourages others
R – Relies on God for everything!

Karen Lynn Coffee

FATHER

F – Fulfills responsibilities
A – Advises with wisdom
T – Teaches life skills
H – Helps others
E – Encourages everyone
R – Respects his family and others

Karen Lynn Coffee

MY LORD AND SAVIOR, JESUS CHRIST

Gentle as a summer's breeze
Yet strong as a mighty oak
Special is he, my Lord and Savior, Jesus Christ
The eagle bows down to him
Roses join to make a regal crown upon his head
The sun at his command graces his shadow

Karen Lynn Coffee

LORD, GIVE ME DIRECTIONS

Lord, give me directions
For life's daily turns
And give me the courage to continue to learn.
I humbly ask for your guidance in all that I do
So I will be a better servant to you

Karen Lynn Coffee

THE GIFTS (1 CORINTHIANS 12)

I am WISDOM, to help you advise others with good decisions
I am KNOWLEDGE, to help you share information with others
I am FAITH, to help you give others belief
I am ENCOURAGEMENT, to help you give others strength
I am DISCERNMENT, to help others see things around them
I am PRAYER, to help you reach others
I am ADMINISTRATION, to help you keep things organized
I am TEACHER, to help you show others what to do
I am COUNSELOR, to help you guide others
I am SOOTHER, to help you comfort others
The gifts are a daily blessing from God.

Karen Lynn Coffee

I SAW GOD TODAY

I saw God today . . . as I walked along the path of life
I heard him say "All is well" as I listened to the waters of a
    rushing stream
I felt him guide me as the wind touched my hand and passed
    through my fingers
I heard him whisper "I Love You" through the singing of
    delightful birds
I felt him cover me as the sun shined brightly throughout the day
I saw God today . . . as I walked along the path of life

Karen Lynn Coffee

SCRIPTURE

"You are welcome at my house," the old man said. "Let me supply whatever you need." (Judges 19:20)

He welcomed them and spoke to them about the kingdom of God, and healed those who needed healing. (Luke 9:11)

"Whoever welcomes one of these little children in my name welcomes me; and whoever welcomes me does not welcome me but the one who sent me." (Mark 9:37)

She speaks with wisdom,
    and faithful instruction is on her tongue. (Proverbs 31:26)

Trust in [God] at all times (Psalm 62:8)

He redeemed my soul from going down to the pit,
    and I will live to enjoy the light. (Job 33:28)

Remember the day you stood before the LORD your God at Horeb, when he said to me, "Assemble the people before me to hear my words so that they may learn to revere me as long as they live in the land and may teach them to their children." (Deuteronomy 4:10)

As Jesus was saying these things, a woman in the crowd called out, "Blessed is the mother who gave you birth and nursed you." (Luke 11:27)

In all thy ways acknowledge him, and he shall direct thy paths. (Proverbs 3:6 KJV)

She is more precious than rubies;
    nothing you desire can compare with her. (Proverbs 3:15)

For wisdom is more precious than rubies. (Proverbs 8:11)

Gold there is, and rubies in abundance,
but lips that speak knowledge are a rare jewel. (Proverbs 20:15)

They send forth their children as a flock;
their little ones dance about. (Job 21:11)

At that time Jesus said, "I praise you, Father, Lord of heaven and earth, because you have hidden these things from the wise and learned, and revealed them to little children." (Matthew 11:25)

Jesus said, "Let the little children come to me, and do not hinder them, for the kingdom of heaven belongs to such as these." (Matthew 19:14)

"Whoever welcomes one of these little children in my name welcomes me; and whoever welcomes me does not welcome me but the one who sent me." (Mark 9:37)